How to Motivate Every Employee

D0530822

"In thinking about motivation from a management perspective, it's very important to appreciate this point: You can't motivate people, you can only influence what they're motivated to do."

"When you look at personal growth as a motivator, you change the way employees think about their work, you help them become more capable, and you give them a meaningful purpose in coming to work."

"A manager's goal must be to help create a truly 'motivating organization,' one that inspires each employee to do his or her very best every day—particularly when the manager isn't looking."

How to Motivate Every Employee

✔ 24 Proven Tactics to Spark Productivity in the Workplace

ANNE BRUCE

MCGRAW-HILL

New York Chicago San Francisco Lisbon
London Madrid Mexico City Milan New Delhi
San Juan Seoul Singapore Sydney Toronto

How to Motivate Every Employee: 24 proven tactics to spark
productivity in the workplace

Anne Bruce

ISBN 13: 978- 0-07711619-4
ISBN 10: 0-07-711619-4

 Professional

Published by:
McGraw-Hill Publishing Company
Shoppenhangers Road,
Maidenhead,
Berkshire, England, SL6 2QL
Telephone: 44 (0) 1628 502500
Fax: 44 (0) 1628 770224
Website: www.mcgraw-hill.co.uk

Reprinted 2007

British Library Cataloguing-in-Publication Data
A catalogue record of this book is available from the British Library.

McGraw-Hill books are available at special quantity discounts. Please
contact the corporate sales executive.

Printed in Great Britain by Cromwell Press Ltd, Trowbridge,Wiltshire

Contents

How to Motivate Every Employee

☑ How to Motivate Every Employee

How to Motivate Every Employee is a small but powerful book written to help managers like you utilize in your career the actions and motivational success strategies of world-class business icons, such as Disney, SAS Institute, Virgin Management Limited, Levi Strauss, Starbucks, Four Seasons Hotels, Capitol One, and more. In addition, there are creative, timely, and immediately applicable tips, tools, techniques, and suggestions—all presented in bite-size chunks—guaranteed to keep you and your employees from falling victim to mediocrity and complacency.

But, ultimately, none of these principles and innovative ideas will be worth anything unless you can translate them into fast action steps that affect your employees' behaviors today—right now! This book allows you to do just that.

Your expert skills and talents have gotten you this far. Now, let this handy, user-friendly book help

you apply the fast facts and quick guidelines to becoming even more successful and effective—as a motivating manager!

I believe in the power and the influence that today's manager or supervisor can have on employee motivation. With the right set of techniques, like the ones included in this book, you can reawaken and revive the spirit in your organization. Not only that, you can inspire all those around you by creating an environment in which employees will tap their own motivational energy and perform their best work.

It's my hope that you will find *24 Ways to Motivate Every Employee* an invaluable workplace tool and resource that you'll refer to again and again. This is a book about managers creating an environment in which their employees feel passionate about doing their jobs and putting the best of themselves into those jobs. I hope you'll feel passionate about the information in this book as well.

"Motivation is about cultivating your human capital. The challenge lies not in the work itself, but in you, the person who creates and manages the work environment."

☐ ~~Motivation isn't your~~ problem

☑ Build a motivated workforce

Here's the million-dollar question: Who would want to be influenced and inspired by you? If you cannot answer this question, then you have no business managing anyone. As a professional speaker and corporate trainer, I have asked this question of thousands of managers and leaders across America and abroad, and you'd be surprised how difficult this question can be for some managers and supervisors to answer. Oftentimes the response is simply a stunned hush.

Here's why being able to answer this question is so important. Managers can't really do anything or be effective in their jobs, if their employees aren't motivated to perform well. So as a manager or supervisor, it's imperative that you continually look for ways to engage your people and rouse their

enthusiasm and commitment to the organization and its goals.

The fact is that people are motivated to do what is in their best interests. Your goal as a manager, then, is to help employees identify their welfare with that of the organization. When this happens, employees will naturally feel motivated to work hard, because it is in their best interest to do so.

All this is another way of saying that motivation is intrinsic. It's what drives us to accomplish our desired ends. Whatever we do, it's always because we believe it will fulfill some present or future personal goal or desire.

Contemplate this. When have you been most excited about your work? For most people that excitement comes from being involved with projects that were near and dear to us—projects we took personally, or in which we believed we could really make a difference and accomplish something for ourselves and others. By helping your employees to identify closely with the job they are doing, you will begin to reap the rewards of intrinsic motivation at work.

And when was the last time you thought about really trying to "turn on" your organization? You're the manager, right? Isn't that your job? Yes, but today motivation needs to be everyone's responsibility. As a manager, it is your job to help build a truly "motivating organization," one that inspires employees to do their very best every day.

Understanding that the role you play as a leader and manager of people is one of extreme importance, here are three key points to help build that motivating organization:

Know why your employees would want to be motivated by you: When you can answer this important question, you will be better equipped to engage workers in their jobs more effectively and influence their behaviors to act more enthusiastically to meet company goals.

Recognize that real motivation is an inside job: People talk about motivation being either intrinsic or extrinsic. But it's really only intrinsic, within each of us. What we refer to as extrinsic motivation is really just external factors, like company perks, bonuses, and pay raises that ultimately affect our intrinsic motivation.

Turn employees on to what's important and meaningful: This requires managers to inspire their followers to be their best, to take risks, to think like entrepreneurs, and to unleash their limitless and synergistic potential.

"Men and women want to do a good job, a creative job, and if they are provided the proper environment, they will do so."
—Bill Hewlett, Co-founder, Hewlett-Packard

☐ ~~They do it for you~~

☑ They do it for themselves

As a manager, if you really want to influence people's motivation, you have to uncover their reasons for doing things. You have to question their purposes and their causes. People aren't going to be truly motivated for *your* reasons and objectives. Employees ask themselves, "What's in it for me?" Knowing this upfront, it's your responsibility to find out what your employees' motives are, then help them connect those motives to your organization's goals and activities. When you do this, you also will be positively affecting each worker's performance on the job.

How do you know that you are doing this well? You'll know when your employees start asking the question, "What's in it for *us*?" By looking out for your people and their best interests, your employees will begin to see that looking out for others and the organization as a whole is how they ultimately

look out for themselves. Sure, it can take some time for this to happen, but if you persist, employees will see the light and it will be worth the wait.

Most managers attempt to influence employee motivation using both positive and negative approaches. As a manager or supervisor, it is important that you understand clearly the three very different techniques used to influence the motivation of people in today's workforce, and, thereby, evaluate their pros and their cons. By studying the three primary ways leaders use to influence their workers, you will find greater opportunity to lead and bring about more positive results when it comes to uncovering your worker's intrinsic motivators.

Here's what works and doesn't work in positively influencing employee motivation:

Fear and manipulation don't work very well: When workers are motivated by fear and manipulation, they are not so much trying to achieve something as they are looking to avoid losing their jobs. This approach often leads to resentment of managers by employees, which then undermines communication and cooperation. The results of trying to scare employees to perform also typically won't last and eventually will almost always backfire on the organization and its managers.

The carrot on a stick seldom works well: Also known as incentive motivation—this technique can

also eventually undermine performance. Sure, people will temporarily work harder to get the reward, but what happens afterwards? You will have to keep coming up with new and better rewards—sweeter carrots—because your employees will expect more and more to go beyond the minimum work required.

Set up an approach that promotes personal growth and purpose: What you want to do is help employees appreciate that they have something to contribute and you want to help them do that. When you emphasize personal growth and development as a way to influence employee motivation, not only do you help employees maximize their contribution, you also are improving the productivity of the company. It's a win for everyone.

"Our chief want is someone who will inspire us to be what we know we can be."
—Ralph Waldo Emerson

☐ Don't worry about what drives people

☑ Know what drives people

Managers need to know what drives their employees. Do you?

For starters, if you put people in jobs where they can meet their individual needs while doing the work that's important to the organization, you'll have employees who are more motivated to perform at their best.

Managers have to make work a place where employees feel good about themselves and where the work people do helps them to feel good inside as well. When your employees come to work, they can't turn off their human side, in other words, their human nature. Employees' needs don't shift when they walk through the workplace door. To get people to perform at high levels, you must plug into

their human side, or their human nature, affirm them, and help them meet their own needs.

Start by paying attention. Watch people doing their jobs. What gets them excited? What turns them on? What turns them off? Encourage employees to try out their own methods, provided those methods are compatible with effectively getting the job done.

Next, send out an employee survey about attitudes in the workplace and ask for suggestions for improvements. Once you get this feedback, don't ignore the results. Use the findings to make changes that will improve everyone's working conditions, including yours.

Of course, you can't help every employee meet every need. And there are certain dangers in expecting an employee's job, no matter how gratifying, to constitute his or her entire life. However, there are certain steps that all mangers can take to help their employees meet some, or even several, of their inner desires that will drive them to do their best work and find greater motivation in the process. Here are three main ways to go about doing this more effectively:

Appreciate everyone's uniqueness: By acknowledging to your staff that everyone is unique, you will be demonstrating that you honor and appreciate the individual talents and differences all employees bring to the organization. And who knows, you might even uncover a diamond in the rough.

Brainstorm for greater fulfillment: One great way to brainstorm and, thereby, motivate workers is to set up employee focus groups. By doing this you will begin to discover what employees would like to get from their work. Ask employees to brainstorm ways to make work more fulfilling. Then don't forget to take action and move forward with ideas and suggestions. When you receive employee ideas that are not appropriate, always explain why and hold out for reconsideration at a later time.

Assume that meaningful purpose is important to people: Always assume that things like personal growth and recognition, creativity, and meaningful purpose are as important to your workers as they are to you. Ask employees to describe their ideal job and what they like or don't like about their work and then use what you learn to make work more fulfilling.

"Ultimately, we're talking about redefining the relationship between boss and subordinate."
—Jack Welch, Former CEO, General Electric

☐ ~~Make employees feel like subordinates~~

☑ **Make employees feel like partners**

If you want your employees to be motivated to do their best, and if you want them to be the most valuable asset on your balance sheet, then let them feel and experience ownership in the organization.

The best managers make every employee feel like a business partner. Why? Because when people feel ownership of something, they look out for it, protect it, and pour themselves into it.

One way world-class organizations and their managers help create workplaces alive with entrepreneurial thinking and a sense of ownership (aside from the usual profit-sharing and stock options) is to retitle their employees' positions. For example: Starbucks and TDIndustries refer to their employees as *partners*. Guidant, famous maker of pacemakers,

uses the term *employee-owners*. And LensCrafters, Marriott, W.L. Gore, Publix Super Markets, and Capital One all call their people *associates*.

Making everyone feel like a partner in the business is one way managers empower their people. Here are some other ways you can do the same:

Encourage entrepreneurial thinking: This goes beyond profit sharing and stock options. It's about the attitude instilled in others by you, the manager. Instilling an entrepreneurial mindset requires employees to think like business owners, not employees. The term also conveys a sense of feeling joint ownership and caring about the success of the business and happiness of its people. When employees feel like entrepreneurs, they're motivated to take exceptional pride in their work because they are treated like business partners, not hired help.

Explain how the business is run: Help employees better understand what's going on outside the walls of your department. When employees know how they fit in and the difference they make, they can do their work more intelligently. Give employees information about the organization's history to help establish a greater sense of pride and identity. Instruct employees on how to read the company's annual report, if one is available. Point out the CEO's message to help clarify organizational goals, mission, vision, and progress. Encourage employees

to identify things they can do to contribute directly to achieving the organization's strategic goals. Then let them act on their ideas.

Help employees feel as if they own the business: If you want your employees to put more of themselves into their work, help them find more of themselves in the work they do. Here's the key: if you want your employees to be motivated to perform at their highest levels, then help them gain more control of their jobs; help them feel as if they belong to a community, and most of all, as if they own the business!

"It's surprising how much you can accomplish, if you don't care who gets the credit."
—Abraham Lincoln

☐ ~~Keep employees in the dark about operations~~

☑ Show employees how the business operates

To succeed in today's business environment, your employees need to know far more about the business than just how to do their jobs. They need to know how it operates.

Influential managers must take the responsibility to help workers better understand the entire organization, gain a clearer perspective on just how the business operates, analyze the competition, learn to take risks, and inspire innovative thinking.

As a manager, you understand how your organization operates and manages its finances. That's your job. So you might not realize what it's like to work without knowing how every person and every job impacts the bottom line. When your employees learn how the organization runs and how it spends

and brings in the money, they become more motivated to help make a difference.

Start by arranging for a business basics training program for all workers. There are several on the market that can be customized to your organization's needs. These programs may use a game format to explain how your organization operates and how it makes and loses money. This can be an enjoyable and fun way to teach employees the business of being in business. And here are a few other suggestions to get people moving on understanding business basics:

Talk money: Share the monthly departmental profit-and-loss statements with your employees. This can quickly help workers to better understand how their jobs and specific duties fit into the overall workings of the organization, their neighborhoods, and even their communities. Take time to analyze scenarios that show the impact one person has on the entire organization. This can be a real eye-opener! The point here is to help your employees see how one person's attitude and behavior might directly impact the organization's bottom line, potential pay raises, bonuses, profit sharing, and so on.

Encourage "open-book managing": The idea of *open book management* has become quite popular. This concept involves sharing the organization's financial data and operational strategies with

employees and then showing them specifically what they cost and what value they add to the organization. Some companies go as far as to post everyone's salaries! A good resource for learning about this approach is the 1992 book, *The Great Game of Business*, by Jack Stack. Information is also available on the Internet at http://greatgame.com.

Help people see the big picture: By showing your employees how to see the big picture and understand the monetary domino effect of every action they take, you instill in them an entrepreneurial mindset that creates a motivated organization. Your purpose here is to develop smarter, more skilled, and highly motivated employees who understand their role in helping the organization succeed, today and into the future. Helping your employees to see the big picture, and not just a myopic view of their specific tasks, can help make that happen.

"Trust—the glue that binds followers and leaders together."

—Warren Bennis

☐ ~~The competition is irrelevant~~

☑ Know your competition

When employees pull together to compete in the marketplace, their level of motivation rises proportionately when they understand just who and what they are competing against. Nothing brings a team together like the challenge of performing at higher levels than its competitors and then helping the organization grow as a result.

Is having your employees know more about the competition dangerous? Possibly—especially when it comes to unveiling such information as employee incentive plans, salaries, and other perks. But remember, the point of having your workers get to know the competition is so that you, as the manager, can use this information to take specific steps to make your company a better place to work. The ultimate goal, of course, is to help create a work environment where employees feel motivated by

much more than incentive plans or slightly higher wages.

Helping employees to better understand the competition doesn't necessarily require taking a "rah-rah" attitude either, as if organizations were high-school football teams. This is just another way to help your employees get the big picture because your competitors are a part of that picture.

You will get to know your competition by researching what they are doing and then using that information to improve your own organization. In that spirit, here are some ways both you and your employees can learn a bit more about your competitors.

Help employees to compete in the marketplace: Show your employees how to compete more effectively in the marketplace by encouraging them to learn more about your industry and staying current with industry changes. Budget for employee membership in your industry's professional associations and then give people an opportunity to read their trade publications. Encourage employees to copy and distribute industry news, overviews, and relevant case studies (in some cases you may need permission from the publisher to do so). Suggest employees join Internet discussion groups on subjects dealing with your industry and its management in general.

Start competitor files: Put someone in charge of obtaining the competitor's promotional literature; then have someone investigate their Web site and obtain a copy of their annual report, if possible. In addition, a competitor file should include copies of advertisements, profiles of top executives, and the organization's awards and recognition. Assign a team to take it all a step further and determine the competition's strengths and weaknesses in the marketplace, market share, and global reach.

Know your competitors and how you measure up against them: A quick and easy way to do this is to have your employees simply ask your customers to evaluate how your organization measures up to the competition. Tell them to be specific. Find out what your customers have to say about your competitor's pricing, customer care programs, product quality, etc. Have employees document the feedback and use this as a basis for internal improvements within your department.

"Next to knowing all about your own business" the best thing is to know all about the other fellow's business
—John D. Rockefeller, Founder, Standard Oil

☐ ~~Punish risk taking~~

☑ **Encourage intelligent risk taking**

Have you ever asked yourself, "Why aren't more of my employees willing to take risks?" Perhaps it's because the few times they tried and things went wrong, they were either disciplined or perhaps even fired. Even when employees succeed at something risky, with a pat on the back for the result, they may also get chastised for taking the initiative. After all, there are channels and chains of command, assigned responsibilities, managers paid to take risks, and so on. Even in more recent years, management has sent out a mixed message to employees: *We want you to feel empowered and take risks—just don't screw up or you're out of here!*

Let's face it, everyone makes mistakes. The best managers know that, but they also recognize that developing a risk-taking mentality is part of helping employees develop an entrepreneurial approach in

their work—and that's motivating! So it is important for you as a manager and leader to support, encourage, and reward intelligent risk-taking behaviors.

The only way to get better is to try new things and organizations that don't innovate stagnate. They may even go out of business.

So how can you create a culture that encourages employees to take intelligent risks and feel comfortable doing so? Here are some ideas to consider:

Tell employees risk is a four-letter word for success: Creative and calculated risk-taking can improve any organization. That means that managers and supervisors should help employees try new ways of doing their work, of experimenting to make improvements, and encourage and support them in taking those risks. And what if things don't work out as planned? That's OK because it means they're trying new things. And sometimes things don't work out. When employees are allowed to be human and make mistakes, the recognition for having taken the risk is what they'll remember.

Empower employees to take risks: Do this by allowing employees to take an active role in decision-making that involves risk. As a leader, you can set the example by trying new things. Demonstrate to employees how to evaluate whether or not to take a risk. Look for the critical issues, assess opportunities against objective criteria to determine the

potential return, then decide whether the risk is worth it and if the organization can stand behind whatever results.

Encourage risk-taking behavior as a learned behavior: Risk-taking is something we learn over time, one step at a time. Remind your employees that there is risk in much of what we do in our daily lives, whether that's getting married, having a baby, buying a house, changing jobs, buying a new car, or moving to another city. The more risks we learn to take over time and the greater those risks become, the easier it is to take on a risky situation that has potential and payoff for the entire organization and its people.

"Not failure, but low aim, is crime."
—James Russell Lowell

☑ Inspire creative and innovative thinking

When you find an organization that survives and thrives over time, it's usually because managers like you have learned how to adapt to their changing circumstances and sometimes even keep ahead of the changes taking place around them. Managers who encourage creativity and innovative thinking among their people are natural-born motivators.

Start by addressing and eliminating any fears employees may have about creative thinking. Some people, for example, don't think they're capable of being creative. Others tend to focus on areas of practicality, analyzing and judging ideas as quickly as they arise. Let your employees know that it's time to lighten up and not to assume that something won't work because nobody's tried it. Have your employees suspend critical judgment when someone presents what may seem to be an off-the-wall or different kind

of idea than what's been proposed in the past. Have employees concentrate on how they can make new ideas work and not what's wrong with them.

Motivating managers pride themselves on providing a free and open environment that inspires employees to offer whatever ideas and suggestions may occur to them—no matter how "impractical" they may seem at first. It's in this type of environment where employees will feel motivated to stretch themselves and use their imaginations to help the organization (and themselves) succeed. Here are some ways to encourage creativity:

Think big. Think virtual: Today, employee brainstorming can be done over long distances through the use of cyberspace auditoriums and virtual conference rooms. Virtual meetings are proliferating and can function just as effectively and synchronously in cyberspace as they can in the office conference room down the hall. Just think, it is now possible for your employees to hash out ideas with colleagues in the UK, get input from other team members in Burlington, Vermont, go over a game plan before a meeting with other employees in Honolulu, and kibitz with a new member of the team in Melbourne, Australia.

Use tools for creative and innovative thinking: Begin by setting aside time to brainstorm with employees and investigate innovative and creative new approaches and ideas. Not only should you sup-

port innovative thinking, but as the manager, you should also help implement new ideas. Make books available to your employees on the subject of creativity, such as *A Whack on the Side of the Head* by Roger von Oech, *Thinkertoys* by Michael Michalko, or *How to Think Like Einstein: Simple Ways to Break the Rules and Discover Your Hidden Genius*, by Scott Thorpe. Through special announcements, newsletters, e-mails, and day-to-day conversations, praise the innovation of your team.

Emphasize positive aspects of innovative solutions: Continually emphasize the positive aspects of innovative solution finding and the disadvantages of always doing the same things in the same way. Refrain from penalizing anyone for trying something new that may end up a big mistake. Instead, encourage others to learn from their mistakes. It's your responsibility to encourage freedom of expression and congratulate those who possess unique, one-of-a-kind creativity and out-of-the-box thinking skills.

"There is nothing that is a more certain sign of insanity than to do the same thing over and over and expect the results to be different."
—Albert Einstein

☐ Ignore the link between motivation and performance

☑ Affirm the link between motivation and performance

As a leader, you need to know that there is a direct link between employee motivation and employee performance. In fact, it can be a positively outrageous connection depending on the culture of your organization and the enthusiasm and excitement your company's culture instills in its people.

Perhaps you've seen companies like Disney, Saturn, SAS Institute, Southwest Airlines, Starbucks, USAA, Rosenbluth International, and The Ritz Carlton (just to name a few) that always seem to go the extra mile for their customers' satisfaction and happiness and whose employees are upbeat and glad to be working there. And without even thinking

about it, you somehow know there is a direct connection between how those employees perform on the job and just how motivated they are about their work. It's practically palpable—you can feel it! That's because these employees are motivated to do these things, and it shows up in the quality of their work. In other words, if you don't think motivation and performance are connected, think again. Here are three important factors to consider when it comes to linking the motivation of your people to higher levels of performance and productivity:

Know the impact you're having on people: All managers occasionally feel as though they are having little or no impact on the motivation of their employees. Let's face it: you can't always change or control certain factors that affect your employees' enthusiasm for their jobs. Some things, such as working conditions, specific assignments, salaries, and benefits you can provide, but other factors can simply be out of your control. Still, as the manager, you have a direct impact on linking employee motivation to performance. Learn some of the effective techniques that are working for other managers and then try them when they seem appropriate for your employees. Be willing to commit to a strategy so that employees don't feel your approach is simply a "flavor-of-the-week" series of gimmicks. You'll be pleasantly surprised to find that you can influence your employees' motivation and improve their pro-

ductivity and attitudes when you try appropriate, innovative techniques and use them with your own personal style of leadership, business sense, and people skills.

Make sure employees know what performance is: Never assume that your employees will automatically know what you mean by "performance." It's your responsibility to clearly define performance standards for them. You need to think of performance in your own terms and then clearly and precisely explain what that means to your employees. Only then will you be capable of linking performance to motivation successfully.

Tell people what's expected of them and be specific: Here are the questions every manager must be able to answer for every employee: "What's expected of me?" "What is my role as a part of the group and the organization?" "What's considered unacceptable performance?" "What must I do to reach your standards of performance?" Be explicit! The more detailed and explicit the expectations, the greater the chance the employee will meet or exceed them.

"No person who is enthusiastic about his work has anything to fear from life."
—Samuel Goldwyn

☐ ~~Let employees worry about their performance~~

☑ **Help them achieve greater performance**

In the beginning lessons of this book, we focused on helping employees become intrinsically motivated. We also focused on how you as a manager or supervisor can more effectively influence the forces that compel others to do the things they do to the best of their talent. In this lesson and the preceding one, we're shifting our focus to getting employees to take *direction* and then stretch themselves in order to turn motivation into stronger performance and higher productivity. Here are some ways to consider doing this:

Stretch people beyond their perceived limits: Take your employees above and beyond the status quo of just doing the same job the same way. Make their

work challenging, and help them to see the bigger picture and the part they play in it. They may resist if they feel that higher expectations are being imposed on them. Let your employees know that you are simply trying to help them stretch and grow for their own benefit. They will love you for it! You can do this by helping them set individual performance goals that exceed the existing requirements of their jobs. Further, when you can explain how their work adds value to the organization and how what they do affects the work of others, your employees can begin to figure out different ways to improve and grow their talents on their own.

Set standards and be clear: Identify those standards for a particular job and be specific about the outcomes that characterize outstanding as well as unacceptable performance. Involve your employees in doing this. Employees who are involved in developing standards are more likely to discuss the obstacles that might impede their efforts along the way, allowing you to handle those issues head on before things get out of hand. Involved employees are also far more likely to understand the standards and reasons behind them, so you won't have to work so hard to communicate these standards again and again. And these employees are far more likely to accept such guidelines for success and be motivated to meet them to the best of their ability.

Define employees' scope of responsibility: Make sure everyone understands who is responsible for each job activity. When employees know their roles, this reduces confusion and gives them a better sense of how they might work with their fellow employees to meet their individual objectives. Once you've done this, you've set up the next step, which is to help employees broaden the scope of their responsibilities and open new opportunities for them. As an employee responds, you might want to suggest that he or she assume greater decision-making authority on a certain project. But be careful. Your goal is not to heap more work on the shoulders of your employees. They need to know that you genuinely appreciate their efforts and want to provide them with the opportunity to learn more and excel on the job. You want your employees to feel that it is in their best interests to go the extra mile.

"All of us do not have equal talent, but all of us should have an equal opportunity to develop our talent."

—John F. Kennedy

☐ Don't worry about
employee buy-in

☑ Get employees to buy into your ideas—and theirs

The more input an employee can provide about the job he or she is expected to perform, the more likely the employee is to buy into your ideas for how to do it well. When they know you actually care about their performance and are willing to listen to their ideas for improvement, they'll be motivated to accept your suggestions as well.

The term "buy-in" is one that every manager uses at one time or another, but often not in the same way. If you think that getting your employees to buy into a program means somehow compelling them to accept it, you're likely to run into problems. Employees truly buy in when they decide to invest

their individual abilities and energies, as if they were business owners making a financial investment in a joint venture. So give your employees the opportunity to get involved. If you do, they will be motivated to buy into higher standards of performance on every level. Here you can contemplate other ways this can be carried out successfully:

Give employees a role in raising workplace standards or performance: When you include your employees in raising workplace standards or performance levels, they'll eagerly share with you their ideas and suggestions for improving the process. Keep in mind that almost all employees have a strong desire to play a role in raising their own performance expectations and, when allowed to do so, will set the bar higher than you might have anticipated.

Document what you and your employees agree on: Develop a written list of performance standards for meeting and exceeding the expectations you've agreed upon with your employees. Remember, you want your employees to continue to stretch, yet you want to be certain they can attain their goals. This is key in staying highly motivated. Next, be specific about what it's going to take to actually reach those goals, in each area or each job function. Document and then give a copy of those expectations to every employee. At your next employee performance review or upon completion of a project, this docu-

ment will serve as the basis for you and the employee to discuss and measure what was accomplished. Remember, what gets measured is what he or she will be most motivated to do.

Plan a course of action, then get moving: Once the standards are set, review the specific tasks of each person's job. Identify and discuss the areas in which each person is skilled and qualified. Plan a course of action and delegate based on each employee's experience and level of competence. Next, let each employee know that once he or she has started the project and gained greater insight into the intricacies of the job, you will be willing at that point to revise the expectations accordingly. Be sure to keep the goals challenging, yet realistic. Now get moving, but take time to observe and follow up. Don't wait until the end of a project to check in with your employees. Following up is an important way you give your employees the feedback they need concerning their performance as it's happening. It's also a great way to demonstrate that your job as manager is to help each employee succeed—reinforcing their motivation to perform.

"Every manager knows how to count, but smart managers know what counts."

—Anonymous

☐ Don't worry about rewards and recognition

☑ Be clear about rewards and recognition

Let your employees know up front what to expect if they meet or exceed the standards of excellence you've set for them with their help. Be clear about potential rewards for hitting those goals. In other words, let employees know what's in it for them, then plan on them succeeding beyond your wildest imagination. Sure, it may be less expensive for the organization if employees fall slightly short on meeting your expectations, because then you'd be saving on those rewards. But the smartest managers know that success, even when it entails additional expense, breeds greater success and motivation among the ranks.

When your employees do hit the target and meet a standard you've set for them, reward them

immediately. Never stall. By doing this, you help employees directly connect the reward with the behavior and higher performance they've attained.

Never make a promise without a plan to deliver. When that happens, it sends a message to employees that you can't be trusted and that you really don't have faith in them. On the other hand, don't make the promise of rewards the main reason for employees to perform. What you want is for employees to know that rewards are recognition of a job well done and not simply the goal of doing the work.

Think about the people behind the performance. Rewards and recognition should fit the achievement, but also the employee. If you want to reward a telemarketer, for example, he or she may appreciate a weekend getaway with meals and accommodations provided. However, if you are rewarding a traveling sales rep, such a prize may not excite him or her who spends a great deal of time in hotels and restaurants anyway.

Here are some positive forms of reinforcement that aren't expensive and will help get the point across to your employees that you want to recognize a job well done:

Create greater autonomy: This tells employees that you trust them to make decisions that affect their work. It also conveys a sense of additional responsibility.

Increase visibility within the organization: Send an e-mail or memo to others publicly recognizing the good work of someone. When you help increase the visibility of an employee who's done a good job, you're reinforcing that good work by your praise and recognition. If it's in the budget, another way to appreciate a job well done is to provide that person with additional resources, such as a new computer system, software, an assistant, or monies for books and seminars.

Showcase success: Showcasing success often calls for special recognition, like a framed certificate or an engraved plaque or trophy. Sometimes managers like to showcase success on a quarterly basis with "Walk-the-Talk" awards or gift certificates for the team. In some cases, managers let the employees themselves showcase their hard work and special accomplishments by asking them to present a special case study at a prestigious management conference or leadership meeting.

"There are two things people want more than sex and money ... recognition and praise."
—Mary Kay Ash, Founder, Mary Kay Cosmetics

☐ ~~Have low expectations~~

☑ **Always expect the best from employees**

It's actually pretty natural, and almost unavoidable, for managers to form expectations of their workers. Research has found that in an organization, our expectations of others can be tied directly to productivity, profitability, and yes—motivation! If you have high expectations of your employees, you will possess a powerful and effective tool for improving performance and motivation within your organization.

Performance is often a matter of expectations. Managers and supervisors form expectations of others, which then influence how they interact with those people. If you don't expect much from your employees, they will sense that and perform poorly. Why? Because your expectations of them affect their desire to do well. The point is that people naturally try to live up to our expectations of them, or live

down to them, whatever the case may be. So expect the best from your employees and don't be surprised if that's exactly what you get! Here are some ideas on how managers can get the best from their people:

Get what you ask for: Expectations influence behavior. Simply put, if you expect the best from your employees, you will more than likely get it—over and over again. This is especially true if you treat employees as if they can perform and you give them the information and tools they need. That makes it easy for them to feel motivated and deliver what you (and now they) expect.

Take advantage of the Pygmalion Effect: That's the tendency of people to act in ways that are consistent with their expectations. Employee performance improves greatly when managers are told beforehand that they are going to be leading an exceptional group of high-potential workers. Because those managers then tend to treat these employees as if they are capable of superior performance, they deliver. Use the Pygmalion Effect, by showing that you are committed to your people and by doing the following: create a high-performance environment, share the rewards of successful performance, and inspire others to higher-level performance.

Create a high-performing, high-producing environment: If you really want to tap into the true motiva-

tion within your employees, you must deliberately create an environment that's conducive to higher levels of employee performance. That means that everyone is clear and focused about the organization's objectives, that the work is stimulating and challenging, that people feel appreciated and respected, that people have the resources they need, and that people help and support one another without being asked to do so.

"Leadership is performance. You have to be conscious of your behavior, because everyone else is."

—Carly Fiorina, CEO, Hewlett Packard

☑ Fire up successful performance

If you really want to fire-up successful performance in your people, then you'll need to inspire them to reach those higher levels of performance and productivity. Great leaders are often inspirational. They seem to have a knack for fostering optimism and belief in a better tomorrow. As a manager or supervisor, you too can create an environment that encourages people to climb to the next level of achievement, satisfaction, and personal excellence.

Do all that you can to show your employees that your actions are meaningful and sincere when it comes to helping them do their best work.

Consider the following strategies: 1) Ask for everyone's input, ideas, and suggestions about the current work environment and how it can be improved. Then publish a plan and let your people put it into action. Now that's motivating! 2)

57

Emphasize your own personal commitment to your team. In other words, you too must be fired up about your work. Always praise the commitment of your staff. 3) Connect the success of your team to the success of the organization. When you practice these strategies, you'll be helping to ensure that management values its people and wants to take actions that will benefit both employees and the organization. Here are some additional ways to fire up employees:

Share rewards: An important goal of any motivation program is to help employees feel that the work itself is the reward. Managers reinforce our natural human motivation when they arrange for employees to enjoy rewards that result from their work. So share the rewards with all those who have contributed to the organization's success. For example, when an employee or group of employees improves a process or saves the company money, share those benefits with them. The plan may include a percentage of the savings or a flat bonus.

Recognize and praise them: Besides pay, there are other ways to share in the rewards of successful performance. For example, you may be amazed at how employees respond to a simple compliment for work well done. It's best to compliment a person face to face, then follow up by sending him or her a letter or e-mail of appreciation. And in this day and

age of technology-generated correspondence, a handwritten card or thank-you note is valued even more. Remember to always be specific in your compliments.

Train, train, train: Nothing fires up successful performance among employees more than training. Training people sends out a clear message that says, "You are worth this investment!" Give employees special learning opportunities, both inside and outside of the organization. Always encourage ongoing personal and professional development and watch motivation soar! When employees are exposed to training programs, seminars, e-learning, etc., it tells them that management really values their performance and wants to help them to continually improve their skills. When you do this, make sure you also give employees immediate opportunities to use their new skills. This way the training pays off quickly and people take what they learned seriously.

"The shortest and best way to make your fortune is to let people see that it is in their interests to promote yours"
—Jean de La Bruyere, 17th-century French Writer

☑ Offer incentives and morale boosters

One way managers are discovering how to enrich the workplace is to boost the benefits of working there. The days when benefits packages included nothing more than a health plan and dental coverage are over. Managers like you are getting more and more creative when it comes to providing their employees with uniquely-their-own incentives and morale boosters that contribute to an ever-changing, exciting, and motivating work environment.

Take a fast lesson from some of these world-class companies that are designing their own employee incentives and providing the motivating perks that result in higher performance levels and happier employees!

- Goldman Sachs, New York: When employees work late into the night, the Wall Street firm sends them home in a limo at no cost.

61

- Valassis Communications, Livonia, Michigan: Employees receive "wheels on loan" if their car is in the shop, "you've got it maid" discounts on maid service, and infant car seats to brand new parents.

- MBNA, Wilmington, Delaware: Say "I do" and the firm gives generous wedding gifts to their employees, including limo service on their wedding day, plus $500 and a week of vacation.

- WRQ, Inc., Seattle, Washington: Quirky but true, this integration software provider offers employees a nap room with futons.

- J.M. Smucker, Orrville, Ohio: The famous jam maker enriches the environment with ongoing job rotations to keep employees motivated and interested.

- REI, Kent, Washington: New dads get two weeks paid leave to be with their babies.

- Dell Computer, Round Rock, Texas: Everyone gets a week off at Christmas and 10 paid days a year for personal use.

Here are some thoughts on how you can be creative with incentives:

Be flexible with employees: Did you know that helping your employees strike a life balance keeps employee motivation high? Did you also know that the most requested perk on the job is flexibility? Here's the kind of flexibility employees ask for the most: telecommuting, flex schedules, job sharing, compressed workweek (10-hour days, four days a

week), reduction in summer work hours, and time off to take care of personal matters when necessary.

Motivate without money: Yes, it's possible to motivate workers with little or no money. Here are some ideas: post a thank-you note on an employee's office door, have a day when managers wash their employees' cars, answer someone's telephone for a day, hold morale-building meetings to celebrate successes, leave a card for a lunch date at the employee's discretion, walk around with dinner gift certificates that can be handed out on the spot, assign a parking spot for an entire month, give two consecutive Fridays off, buy someone flowers, make a contribution to someone's favorite charity.

Walk the talk: Be the role model for what you expect in others. Also, convey your enthusiasm and remind others that problems can be overcome. Always recognize people who conquer obstacles to achieve results. Focus on the positive side of new ideas. Meet with people individually or in groups, especially when morale is low. Express your optimism and faith in the team. Concentrate on the small, but significant wins, not just the big successes. Make work fun and celebrate a lot!

"People want to feel what they do makes a difference."
—Frances Hesselbein, President, The Drucker Foundation

☐ ~~Hoard your power~~

☑ **Give your power away**

Let your people be powerful. If you really want to pump them up, then prepare to give your power away.

Even before empowerment became a management buzzword, smart managers were already familiar with the basic principle: when workers feel strong, confident, and capable, they can accomplish more. Those same managers also know that when workers feel unappreciated or insignificant to the overall operation, and when they lack responsibility and authority, they tend to perform down to low management expectations. They also tend to whine and complain a lot.

That's why the most motivating managers give their power away over and over again. Sure it's unconventional and many managers resist doing this because they like holding all the power. But think about it for a minute. You're not there as a manager to hold the power. That's just a resource—

a means toward an end. Your responsibility as a motivating manager is to use your authority to get results and to help your employees perform better. So if giving your power away helps to improve performance, then by all means, that's exactly what you should be doing.

When you give your power away, you are allowing your employees to share your responsibility and authority. They find greater motivation in their work and little by little you will free yourself from the burden of using whips, carrots, or other extrinsic forces to try to influence them and their behaviors. Here are some additional lessons to achieving that same goal:

Help employees accept responsibility for motivation: When employees rely on themselves to stay motivated, rather than on others, they're accepting self-responsibility. And when they accept responsibility for themselves, they understand that they also have responsibility for their success. To encourage self-responsibility for motivation, give employees carte blanche responsibility for achieving a specific task or project to make it their own, and give the full authority to do it their way. This will unleash tremendous energy and motivation among your people. Remember, one of the greatest de-motivators is to assign responsibility to someone and then turn around and tell them how to do the job. Top managers won't make this mistake.

Let the people take the power: Smart managers know the importance of releasing the power within each employee so that he or she can do their best work. When your people take the power, you will be giving them the authority and responsibility to do their jobs efficiently and effectively, on their own. "People have the power" has long been the credo at the famous jeans maker, Levi Strauss & Co., and has helped sustain the company through the fringed '60s and bell-bottomed '70s, to the total reinvention of the jeans culture at the turn of the century.

Redefine your role as manager: To do this, start by enlarging every employees' circle of influence. Then increase signature authority whenever possible. Don't let employees feel restricted by their titles or positions. Everyone's a leader. Define jobs more broadly, leaving room for creativity and autonomy. Eliminate cumbersome employee rules and policies. And always support good judgment and common sense. Remember Nordstrom's employee hand-book, which simply states: *Rule #1: Use your good judgment in all situations. There will be no additional rules.*

"If you want someone to do a good job, give them a good job to do."
—Frederick Herzberg, Management Theorist

☐ Discourage a sense of accountability

☑ Encourage accountability at all times

What's the best way to encourage accountability among your employees? By helping them understand and appreciate the role they play in the big organizational picture.

There's a saying that should make every manager think: "No individual raindrop ever considers itself responsible for the flood." And on a more positive note: "No individual raindrop ever can take credit for the flowers." It's lots of raindrops working together, each making its contribution.

People who do extraordinary things do so because they are accountable to themselves first. It's definitely not just to get a raise or promotion. What pushes each and every one of us to go the extra mile or to climb the highest mountain? It's self-motiva-

tion—motivation that comes from within one's heart and mind, motivation that holds each person accountable. There truly is no greater human force. Here are some ideas for plugging into that:

Encourage employees to believe in themselves: Whatever actions you may take as a manager, your ultimate goal should be to help all of your employees believe in themselves and believe that they can accomplish what they set out to do. Help your employees accept a sense of accountability for their work. This will not only guide them, but inspire them as well. When a woman by the name of Ffyona Campbell set out to walk 16,088 kilometers across Africa from Cape Town to Tangiers, it amazed everyone. When asked why she was doing it, she replied, "Because I said I would." When asked who she said it to, she answered, "Myself." Ffyona believed in herself, and it was that inner belief and confidence that inspired her to take on the more treacherous terrain on foot and alone. Her self-motivated and extraordinary efforts earned her the title "The Greatest Walker of Them All."

Help others bridge the gap to achieving goals: Staying self-motivated and accepting responsibility is the bridge between setting goals and reaching them. It's always the driving force behind people's achievements. Here are two effective ways to help your employees bridge the gap to achieve their

goals. One, help employees face fear. Encourage employees to openly discuss their fears and what scares them most and then take action in spite of those fears. When employees start moving toward their goals, their fears and anxieties will soon dissipate and confidence will begin to strengthen. Two, help employees focus on the end result. Help them visualize what success might look like and then drive toward it.

Hold employees accountable: Being accountable means taking responsibility for your actions and their outcomes. Real accountability goes beyond the performance of a task. It means they feel responsible for their work and for the results they achieve. Here are some tips for holding your employees accountable: develop a list of mutually acceptable performance criteria; connect expectations to employee reviews and put expectations in writing beforehand; establish rewards for success and consequences when a job is done poorly; make excellence the only option and demonstrate a low tolerance for mediocrity.

"We must exchange the philosophy of excuse—what I am is beyond my control—for the philosophy of responsibility."
—Barbara Jordan, lawyer and former member of congress

~~Don't worry about building trust~~

☑ Build trust for a better tomorrow

Motivation is partly based on a vision of hope—the hope for success from our efforts and for a better future for ourselves. In other words, *what life could be*. When we believe in the possibilities, for ourselves and for our employees, a brighter tomorrow opens up.

As a manager, one of the most important things you can do for your people is to give them hope. Not just hope by itself, but hope that offers direction, believability, and genuine encouragement. When people have a good sense about their future, it reinforces their enthusiasm and commitment to the work in which they're involved. It's motivating. It says there is a payoff to the individual for doing well. Here are other ways managers work toward building a better tomorrow for their employees:

Understand the phenomenon of human potential:
Potential is something that may or may not be fully
developed in people. Whatever people's potential
might be, they won't know unless they have a
chance to develop it. And that's where you as a
leader come in. Take time to rent and watch the
movie, *Phenomenon*, starring John Travolta. The
film sends a profound message about our untapped
potential and is poignantly delivered near the end
of the movie by Travolta's character, George Malley,
who says, "I am what everyone can be. I'm the pos-
sibility and anyone can get there." You can help
unleash that possibility by encouraging people to
try new things and take on new responsibilities.

Build trust: Trust is an essential element in man-
aging people and building a high-performing orga-
nization. It's the foundation upon which all rela-
tionships are built. According to Tom Peters,
"Technique and technology are important. But
adding trust is the issue of the decade." Peters sug-
gests that managers must take a "high-tech and high-
trust" approach, putting the issue of trust at the top
of the agenda and treating it like a "hard issue," not
a "soft issue." If employees feel you don't trust them
to do their jobs correctly, they'll be reluctant to do
much without your approval. On the other hand,
when they feel trusted that you can believe they'll
do the right things, they'll naturally want to do
things well and be deserving of your trust.

Show employees they are worthy of your trust:
When you put your trust in others, you're sending a strong message that says, "I think you're trustworthy." This tells people that you have faith in their ability and competence and you believe they've got what it takes to do the job. Trust is a prerequisite for building confidence in people. Some managers don't discuss the issue of trust, or they use the word in very limited contexts, often almost negatively. For example, "Now, Matt, I trust you to do this right" means "Don't screw up, Matt." And, "We're trusting you to do your best, Jane" really sends the message, "We're not sure what's happening here, so we're just hoping that you can somehow pull this off." These, so-called, expressions of "trust" are unlikely to reassure Matt or Jane. Show your trust in employees by allowing them to think for themselves, ask questions, and make their own decisions. Those are the "real" expressions of trust employees can sense and believe. This is how smart managers show employees that they are worthy of their trust.

"The trust that we put in ourselves makes us feel trust in others."
—François de la Rochefoucauld,
17th-century French writer

☐ ~~Morale is out of your control~~

☑ Boost morale

Morale has to do with the enthusiam and commitment people bring to their jobs everyday. It affects their motivation to perform. Low morale = low motivation. High morale = high motivation. It may not be quite that simple, but there is a direct correlation between morale and motivation.

Every organization depends on the relationships that its people have among one another. A high-morale workplace needs to be built on the concepts of trust and integrity. But it's not enough for you to trust your employees. They've got to trust you as well. Employees want to believe that their managers are looking out for their best interests. And the way that happens is for them to experience it everyday on the job. The great thing about this is that the employees (nearly all of them, anyway) will want to reciprocate, looking out for your and the organization's best interests.

Remember that your people are your greatest and most valuable resource. You may have hired them for their aptitudes, but the key to higher performance lies in their attitudes. The more you can do to build a high-morale workplace, while instilling trust in your employees, the more motivated they will be. Let's look at some ways you can do this throughout your organization:

Do what you say you will do: Be short on promises and long on fulfillment. Nothing builds trust more than having your words and actions match. Good intentions aren't enough. Tell your employees you care, and then match that up with deeds that demonstrate it everyday. High morale will follow naturally.

Let integrity be the highest form of intelligence in your organization: Integrity has been described by some as the highest form of human intelligence. Integrity is not only an expansion of human honesty and trustworthiness, it is what remains when we strip away all of our credentials and reputation. It's our moral fiber and conscience, our principal beliefs and values. And it is also another characteristic of the high-morale workplace.

Be truthful and show your human side: Do you believe in what you are conveying to others? Are you true to yourself? Do you lead by example and do the right things in accordance with your values? You

can't be a good manager if you're acting in ways that are inconsistent with who you really are and what you believe. Be truthful with people and don't be afraid to show your human side. It's OK to share your mistakes, your hopes, and your dreams. Be down to earth and straightforward with people. Employees will respect and appreciate your honesty and your humanity—two more characteristics of the high-morale workplace.

"We must do more than simply do things right—we must also do the right things."
—Excerpt from "Our Values," Pfizer Pharmaceutical

☐ ~~Fun doesn't belong at work~~

☑ Make it fun to make it motivating

The data are in and the results are clear! There is a direct correlation between fun on the job and employee productivity, creativity, morale, satisfaction, retention and, yes, you guessed it, profitability—not to mention greater customer satisfaction and a host of other benefits. For example, having fun at work helps to alleviate stress and tension, improve communication, ease conflict, unite people, eliminate boredom and fatigue, and create lots of positive energy!

In other words, people who work in an enjoyable and fun-filled workplace come to see their jobs as a place to fulfill many different needs, reinforcing their motivation to perform at a higher level.

You can certainly train people to do just about anything. But the key to real success and to leading a motivated workforce is having people who really *want* to do their jobs and who love to come to work. These people enlighten the workplace and energize their co-workers. That's the big difference having fun at work can make. If you think you're ready to take life a little less seriously and begin enjoying the benefits of a more fun and happier workplace, consider the following:

Instigate the "fun"damentals of motivation: Let's say you're convinced that it's good business to loosen up and create a fun and more enjoyable workplace—great! But suppose you just don't know how to go about it? Here are a few tips for setting up the "fun"damentals of motivation where you work:

- Laugh with people, not at them.
- Lighten up. Don't take yourself too seriously.
- Think with a sense of humor.
- Adopt a fun and playful attitude.
- Plan to have a good time every single day.
- Help others see the lighter side of things.

Need more help? Check out *301 Ways to Have Fun at Work*, by Dave Hemsath and Leslie Yerkes and *Get Weird!* by John Putzier.

Know the connection between fun and the bottom line: Do you want to reduce absenteeism, promote greater job satisfaction, boost employee perfor-

mance, increase productivity, and suffer less down-time? By encouraging a fun work environment, these will be just a few of the bottom-line benefits you can expect. Also, take time to study some of the world's most fun organizations. Here are a few fun companies to check out: Rock and Roll Hall of Fame and Museum (Cleveland, Ohio), Virgin Management Limited, Southwest Airlines, Disney, and Ben & Jerry's. And here's one more tidbit to consider: a survey of business school deans and business executives revealed that humor plays a significant part in the operation of a healthy, successful business.

Recognize the power of fun: Fun, laughter, humor—it's all cleansing. It unites us with everyone else who is having fun. It can make it nearly impossible to feel lonely or left out. When we share a laugh, we enjoy the laugh, but we also enjoy the sharing. Fun is motivating because of the pleasure it creates. So when your employees are feeling a bit down, stressed, tired, or just not in the mood to work up to their abilities, a laugh can make a big difference.

"All I wanna do is have some fun. I got a feeling I'm not the only one."
—Sheryl Crow, Recording Artist

☐ ~~Ignore de-motivation~~

☑ **Attack de-motivators head on**

As a manager, you directly or indirectly impact your employees' self-confidence, their desires, their long-term interests, and their overall ability to love what they do for a living. That's a lot of pressure on any manager to get it right.

This book is full of tips and guidelines to help you positively influence the motivation of your employees. But, let's face it. We live in demanding and increasingly negative times. No matter how supportive, motivating, or encouraging you may be as a manager, you're no doubt constantly facing circumstances that negatively influence the motivation of your employees.

So how do you as a leader build and maintain hope in the midst of influences that threaten to de-motivate? Simple. You attack the de-motivators head on. Concentrate on putting your energy into what you *can* do, rather than dwelling on de-motivating

circumstances and making their effects worse. If you do this, you will be better able to combat doom and gloom and confront the adversity that negatively affects the motivation of your employees.

Remember that de-motivators are factors that deflate the motivation bubble. They can be events, management decisions, disappointments, a lack of praise and rewards, and so on. Zeroing in on what's causing your people to feel deflated can help you to attack the de-motivators and keep them at bay. There are three specific areas you need to be aware of in which you can build organizational strength so that your employees can better handle de-motivating situations:

Hire for the best fit: The best way to counter de-motivation is to prevent it, and sometimes the problem can be with the people you hire. There are folks who tend to get de-motivated quite easily or who are just negative in one way or another. Since you can't count on overcoming a person's psychological issues, it's best to avoid hiring such people. Put some time into screening out candidates who seem likely to suffer from motivation problems.

Hold on to your best employees by creating an environment that offers lots of feedback and builds confidence: Losing good people is a definite de-motivator. To avoid that, give your employees accurate and honest feedback and praise. Feedback strengthens

employees and builds confidence, even when it's corrective. Ask your employees how they would like to receive feedback from you. You'll be establishing a foundation that helps to avoid surprises and minimize de-motivating discomfort. Managers who create an environment rich with honest feedback and praise encourage employee cooperation and trust and higher levels of performance and productivity.

Protect people's dignity and self-respect at all times: One of the greatest de-motivators for employees is having their dignity undermined. Create an environment that encourages employees to respect one another. Some tips for doing this: never criticize an employee in front of others; offer corrective feedback only in private; never point a finger at someone—it's demeaning and unprofessional; never use a condescending tone of voice; never attack someone personally; focus on professional behaviors and performance only; and finally, if you expect others to respect your sense of dignity, you should show them the same respect.

"There's only one way to know how strong employee motivation is throughout your company—ask the people who actually work there. If the de-motivators are seeping in, then it's time to put the kibosh on any and all de-motivators in a hurry!"
—Anonymous

☐ Don't ~~worry about~~ employee retention

☑ Retain your employees

For a manager, it all comes down to keeping the people who keep your business in business. Is your culture one that turns people on and gets them excited about coming to work? Are all employees treated with dignity? Do their jobs have a meaningful purpose? That's important to retaining your best employees. It's only natural that people want to work and stay at a place that embraces caring and respect for others.

When you hire and invest in people, you create a valuable asset, and you want to hold on to them and keep them feeling motivated. So what have we found out about doing this? Research and surveys have proven time and again that it's not about the money, titles, or shareholder value. And let's face it,

you may not have much power to control those aspects anyway. It all comes back to creating an environment where people want to work and will do just about anything to get hired and keep their jobs.

Managers who understand this work toward building a reputation in their organization that says, "Everyone wants to work here." The Men's Wearhouse is a good example of high employee retention. New hires spend about four days in one of the 30 sessions held yearly at the corporate university. The cost to the company? A cool million. The return on investment? Lower turnover than any of its competitors in the industry. And all managers know that the hiring process is complicated, time-consuming, and filled with uncertainty. Minimize having to do that by holding on to the people you have. Here are some additional pointers and ideas to remember for motivating and retaining your talent:

Know what keeps the people who keep you in business: It comes down to creating an environment where your employees feel right—a culture that suits them—like at Google, one of the Web's most successful and growing search engines. Here employees play roller hockey during work hours, bring their dogs to work, and eat lunch and dinner for free in the company café. The result? Employees work long, hard hours and love their jobs.

Understand the reasons employees stay: It's not about the money. Top performers want to work in a pleasant and progressive environment where they feel valued and respected. Money is secondary.

Let values and attitude be your guide: What people know is far less important than what they are. Organizations like Nordstrom, Rosenbluth International, Nucor Steel, and JetBlue believe that a truly successful organization is based on finding people with the right mindset, values, and attitude, not simply experience. Hiring people whom you *want* to keep is an important step in building a culture that makes people want to stay with you.

"Recruit your people everyday, even though your crew is already on board."

—Mike Abrashoff, Founder,
Grassroots Leadership LLC, Boston, MA

☐ Teams don't care about emotion

☑ Put heart and soul into your team

In this global society in which we work, we tend to first learn about such things as business operations, finance, marketing strategy, productions, customer service, and so on. That can mean that as managers we sometimes neglect the fact that, at their very core, organizations are about people and the relationships they develop in working together.

It's the people and the teams they create that turn individual employees into a community of people working together to achieve individual and shared goals. And it's because managers care about their people that this actually becomes possible. There's a saying that goes: "People don't care how much you know, until they know how much you care." Why? Because when you care about your employees, you

create an atmosphere where they care about you and about each other. It turns on their motivation to perform well and to want to improve.

If you genuinely care about your employees and show them, you'll be meeting their basic need to be cared about. You'll be motivating them with heart and soul. And it's that special feeling of reassurance that will help them find greater motivation to work harder and smarter.

Inspire motivated teamwork: Making a difference and collaborating with others to achieve a goal are two of the most powerful motivators for accomplishing challenging work. Put these two things together and you have the potential for a high-performing team. Do all you can to show your appreciation for the contributions an employee makes and by being a leader who promotes and facilitates teamwork.

Lead from the heart: The word "encouragement" has as its root the Latin word cor, which means "heart." When you encourage employees, you actually give them heart. You lead them with feeling. When Barbara Walters interviewed General Norman Schwarzkopf following the Gulf War, she asked him how he would most like to be remembered. His answer was from the heart: *That he loved his family. That he loved his troops. And that they loved him.* Motivating leadership is an affair of the heart

and such leaders care about their employees and their organizations. Employees will naturally and positively respond to this.

Encourage team spirit: Smart managers know that team spirit unifies. Transforming a group of individuals into a team provides unification and a common sense of interest and direction. Keep in mind that as the manager, you are setting the tone. Your actions and attitudes directly affect the environment in which your team must perform. Here are some suggestions for encouraging team spirit:

- Give teams a clearly defined goal and purpose.
- Let the team make its own rules.
- Encourage fun and a sense of humor on the job.
- Give employees the authority to make decisions and act on them.
- Be supportive. Do what you promise to do.
- Let the team find solutions to its problems without intervening.
- Allow team members to make financial decisions and create their own budgets.
- Expect ups and downs. Some phases of a project will run more smoothly than others.
- Let the team set up a reward system.

"Coming together is a beginning; keeping together is progress; working together is success."
—Henry Ford

☐ Human potential isn't your problem

☑ Unleash the power of human potential

Did you know that your brain's capacity is practical-ly unfathomable? In terms of its intricacies and power, the brain surpasses even the latest technologies. It can actually process up to 30 billion bits of information per second through the equivalent of more than 6,000 miles of computer wiring. The fuel that fires up your brain is pretty simple: oxygen in the blood and a little glucose, and bingo, you've got energy. And without energy, there can be no synergy in your organization.

When people feel tired or listless, they don't accomplish nearly as much as they're capable of accomplishing. When you work on increasing your employees' energy, you help them move toward a bet-ter life working together. That's what synergy really means—working together. It's a simple, natural con-

cept that managers like you are learning to adopt in their business practices. As management experts stress the importance of "smart work" and "intellectual capital," managers and supervisors are realizing the importance of these synergistic qualities and the benefits they can produce within the team's structure.

This book has given you lots of ways for getting the best from your employees. The guidelines and tips offered were meant to get you thinking—thinking about the potential that lies within you and all of your employees, the phenomenal power of all that intelligence, creativity, curiosity, and energy. As a manager and leader, it is imperative that you make the most of all that potential around you. The results will be well worth your efforts, as the synergy you develop will keep growing, building, and motivating for a long time to come. In the words of Ralph Waldo Emerson, "Make the most of yourself ... for that is all there is of you." Here are some more ways that managers unleash the power of human potential in their employees:

Train 'em: The saying goes, "Knowledge is power." It is not. What is powerful is how knowledge is used. So what kind of training programs do you provide to help employees gain new knowledge and use it effectively? Training helps employees improve their skills and performance—and it shows in yet another way that you care about them.

Coach 'em: Once you've invested in your employees' learning and development, it's time to

start a coaching program. You go to a lot of trouble to maintain your computers and other equipment. But when it comes to sustaining the motivation of your employees, it's easy to forget that they too must be "maintained." Coaching is an effective way to maintain employee motivation. Here's the definition of the word "coach": "Someone who lends experience, encouragement, and understanding to inspire someone to his or her best performance."

Love 'em: Like the hit song by Tina Turner asks, "What's love got to do with it?" The answer: everything! The truly successful manager is a manager who actually loves his or her people and demonstrates this love by encouraging a loving atmosphere on the job. Simply put, "love" in this context means that you're concerned about your people and their success, that you feel glad when they succeed, and that you are willing to help them out and go the extra distance when they need it. The feeling of a loving and caring work environment is the essence of inspiring motivated teamwork.

"Work can provide the opportunity for spiritual and personal, as well as financial, growth. If it doesn't, then we're wasting far too much of our lives on it."

—James A. Autry, *Love and Profit: The Art of Caring Leadership*

"How important is motivation? It makes all the difference. You may be the most knowledgeable, experienced, talented, and capable manager in the world. But if your employees are lacking in motivation, mediocrity will creep into your organization."

"If you eliminate obstacles that hold back the individuals responsible for the success or failure of a project, you'll create an environment that encourages natural motivation and team spirit."

"Effective managers make every employee feel like a business partner. Why? Because when people feel ownership of something, they feel a strong motivation to look out for it."

The McGraw-Hill Mighty Manager's Series

How to Manage Performance
24 lessons to improve performance
by Robert Bacal
ISBN 13: 978-0-07-711623-1
ISBN 10: 0-07-711623-2

Arms you with proven techniques for inspiring breakthrough productivity levels and infusing both you and your employees' careers with renewed commitment and success.

How to Plan and Execute Strategy
24 steps to implement any corporate strategy successfully
by Wallace Stettinius, D Robley Wood Jr, Jacqueline L Doyle, John L Colley Jr
ISBN 13: 978-0-07-711622-4
ISBN 10: 0-07-711622-4

Provides you with 24 practical steps for creating, implementing, and managing market-defining, growth-driving strategies.

The Handbook for Leaders
24 lessons for extraordinary leadership
by John H Zenger, Joseph Folkman
ISBN 13: 978-0-07-711624-8
ISBN 10: 0-07-711624-0

This precise, no-nonsense rulebook shows you how and why to focus on your core strengths instead of correcting your weaknesses. It outlines the essential competencies and guidelines for effective leadership.

Managing in Times of Change
24 tools for managers, individuals and teams
by Michael Maginn
ISBN 13: 978-0-07-711625-5
ISBN 10: 0-07-711625-9

> Shows how to help your workforce realize the benefits of change
> and flourish within their new environment and responsibilities.

How to Motivate Every Employee
24 proven tactics to spark productivity in the workplace
by Anne Bruce
ISBN 13: 978-0-07-711619-4
ISBN 10: 0-07-711619-4

> Tips for motivating your workforce for their own careers and the
> long-term success of your business.

Dealing with Difficult People
24 lessons to bring out the best in everyone
by Rick Brinkman, Rick Kirschner
ISBN 13: 978-0-07-711620-0
ISBN 10: 0-07-711620-8

> Disarm problem people, find common ground and turn
> conflict into cooperation.

The Sales Success Handbook
20 lessons to open and close sales now
by Linda Richardson
ISBN 13: 978-0-07-711621-7
ISBN 10: 0-07-711621-6

> Outlines a battle-tested program for hearing and understanding
> exactly what your customers have to say and selling solutions
> instead of just selling products.

Project Management
24 lessons to help you master any project
by Gary R Heerkens
ISBN 13: 978-0-07-711731-3
ISBN 10: 0-07-711731-X

Provides you with the fundamental skills of successful project management, from understanding the role to working within budgets and leading a team to understanding the basic tools of project analysis.

Leadership Under Pressure
24 lessons in high performance management
by Danny Cox with John Hoover
ISBN 13: 978-0-07-711730-6
ISBN 10: 0-07-711730-1

This hands-on rulebook shows you how to infuse your company with results driven leadership at every level, especially during difficult times.

About the Author

A former television talk show host and producer for CBS, Anne Bruce has been a featured presenter for the White House, the Harvard and Stanford law schools, and the London Institute of Management. Her motivational programs on leadership, customer service, the power of human potential, and an array of communications topics have been featured at worldwide business conferences, at professional asociations, and in hundreds of corporations, including Coca-Cola, Sprint, Ben & Jerry's, Southwest Airlines, The Southern Company, Lanier Worldwide, Blue Cross/Blue Shield, Paine Webber, Baylor University Medical Center, the American Red Cross, and the Conference Board of Europe.

Anne's books, such as *Perfect Phrases for Documenting Employee Performance Problems* (McGraw-Hill, 2005), *Building a High Morale Workplace* (McGraw-Hill, 2003), *Leaders—Start to Finish: A Road Map for Developing and Training Leaders at All Levels* (ASTD Publishing, 2000), and *Motivating Employees* (McGraw-Hill, 1999), have inspired thousands of people and have been translated into more than a dozen languages worldwide.